Searchlight BOOKS™

Cutting-Edge STEM

Cutting-Edge

Military Tech

Matt Doeden

T0015812

Lerner Publications ◆ Minneapolis

Lerner Publications Company
An imprint of Lerner Publishing Group, Inc.
241 First Avenue North
Minneapolis, MN 55401 USA

For reading levels and more information, look up this title
at www.lernerbooks.com.

Main body text set in Adrianna Regular.
Typeface provided by Chank.

Library of Congress Cataloging-in-Publication Data

Names: Doeden, Matt, author.
Title: Cutting-edge military tech / Matt Doeden.
Description: Lerner Publications : Minneapolis, [2020] | Series: Searchlight books: cutting-edge STEM | Includes bibliographical references and index. | Audience: Grades 4–6. | Audience: Ages 8–11.
Identifiers: LCCN 2019016705 (print) | LCCN 2019017724 (ebook) | ISBN 9781541583450 (eb pdf) | ISBN 9781541576834 (lb : alk. paper) | ISBN 9781541589377 (pb : alk. paper)
Subjects: LCSH: Military art and science—Technological innovations—Juvenile literature.
Classification: LCC U42.5 (ebook) | LCC U42.5 .D64 2020 (print) | DDC 623—dc23

LC record available at https://lccn.loc.gov/2019016705

Manufactured in the United States of America
1-46665-47661-8/19/2019

Contents

Chapter 1

WHAT IS MILITARY TECHNOLOGY?

High above Earth, military satellites hover. Cameras aboard the satellites zoom in on a battlefield, capturing real-time images. On the ground, soldiers use these images to find the enemy. The soldiers load bullets into their high-tech rifles. Overhead, a swarm of tiny drone aircraft soars through the sky. The self-flying drones scan the battlefield and warn soldiers of threats.

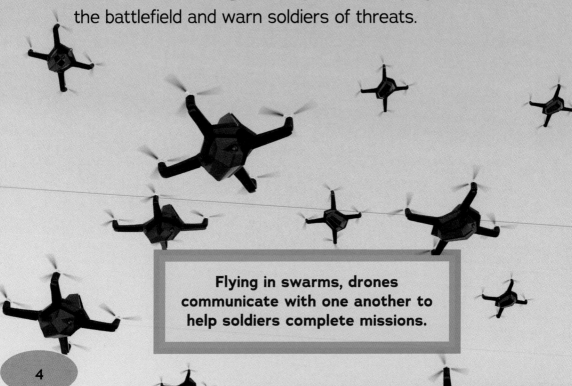

Flying in swarms, drones communicate with one another to help soldiers complete missions.

Submarine drones can be much smaller and lighter than a sub with a human crew like this one.

Hundreds of miles away, another mission plays out at sea. A small ship tracks an enemy submarine. The ship follows the submarine, sending information back to the ship's base as it goes. But neither the ship nor the submarine has a crew. They're both self-steering drones.

Tech in planes and ships lets soldiers monitor everything from enemy movements to weather conditions.

Centuries ago, the side with more soldiers would usually win the battle. But those days are gone. Instead, technology is at the heart of modern military forces. New technology allows soldiers to fight more safely and intelligently than troops did in the past. It's important to have both the right technology and soldiers trained to use it. On the battlefield, this can be the difference between success and failure.

Chapter 2

LAND AND SEA

Technology plays a big part in battles on the ground and at sea. Drone vehicles don't need a pilot, so they can perform missions too risky for humans. Wearable technology such as "smart" glasses lets soldiers access vital information in the field. High-tech weapons can fire with incredible precision.

Robots such as this one (*right*) help soldiers defuse bombs from a distance.

Smart and Stealthy Vehicles

Technology is changing warfare on land. Tanks are big, bulky, and hard to hide. But a new system called ADAPTIV promises to camouflage tanks from infrared sensors. Militaries use infrared sensors to find enemy vehicles. The sensors detect infrared light. This light is similar to heat and invisible to humans. The ADAPTIV system covers tanks in small panels that can change temperature. The panels match the heat of the tank's surroundings, making the tank invisible to infrared sensors.

The ADAPTIV system could help hide ships or helicopters too.

The US Navy tested the *Sea Hunter* by having it sail from California to Hawaii and back.

At sea, the best way to keep sailors safe is to avoid dangerous missions. The *Sea Hunter* does just that. Since the drone ship doesn't need a crew, it saves the US Navy money and prevents risk to sailors. The *Sea Hunter*'s purpose is to search for and track enemy submarines. It can travel thousands of miles and sail for months without refueling.

Drones such as these collect data underwater.

Drone ships aren't just for the surface, either. Life on a submarine can be dangerous. Submarines often get close to enemy ships or bases, and an attack can come at any time. The US Navy will begin to use Orca Extra Large Unmanned Undersea Vehicles. With drone vehicles such as the Orca, the navy doesn't have to put sailors at risk.

Super Soldiers

Soldiers are the backbone of any military. Modern technology makes soldiers stronger, smarter, and tougher. US soldiers carry a lot of gear, from body armor to night-vision goggles. This gear is heavy and weighs them down. But the military is looking at a cool, cutting-edge solution. It's a wearable machine called a robotic exoskeleton.

Carrying a lot of gear means soldiers can tire out quickly.

The lightweight metal skeleton is equipped with many sensors. These sensors work together to help the skeleton match the soldier's movements. The skeleton bears much of the weight a soldier carries. Then soldiers can save their energy for more important tasks.

One day, exoskeletons might provide soldiers armor as well as weight support.

LOOKING AT REAL-TIME DATA, SOLDIERS CAN MAKE MORE INFORMED DECISIONS.

▼

Augmented reality is another new technology that could give soldiers an edge in the field. Special gear shows soldiers key data as they look at a battlefield. This wearable tech lets soldiers access maps, high-quality images, X-ray vision, and more, all without taking their eyes off the battle.

High-Tech Weapons

In battle, close-up combat is especially dangerous. The US Army is developing more long-range weapons to keep soldiers safe. One of these, the Strategic Long-Range Cannon, could hit targets as far away as 1,150 miles (1,851 km). With this range, the cannon could hit distant enemy ships or even planes.

The Strategic Long-Range Cannon will be similar to this gun but bigger.

The latest technology is making military rifles more accurate. Next Generation Squad Weapons will come with built-in night vision. Computers on the rifles will detect conditions such as wind speed, wind direction, and distance from the target. The computers will then help soldiers adjust their aim.

New weapons will help improve soldiers' range and accuracy.

Science Fact or Science Fiction?

New bullets can steer themselves in flight.

That's a fact!

The US military has created a smart bullet that uses a computer to track a moving target. The bullet has tiny fins that allow it to adjust its course while in the air. Even users without military training can hit targets with this bullet.

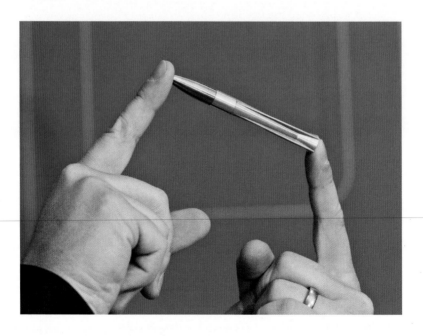

Chapter 3

AIR AND SPACE

Modern militaries often win or lose fights from above the battlefield. Sometimes *way* above! Much of the most amazing military technology flies high above the battle, even reaching all the way into space.

The US military spends billions of dollars to develop the most advanced aircraft.

The F-35 Lightning II can go supersonic. That means it flies faster than the speed of sound!

Amazing Aircraft

The F-35 Lightning II might be the most high-tech airplane ever made. The F-35 entered military service in 2015. It can serve as a fighter, a bomber, or a spy plane. Its stealth technology makes it hard for enemies to spot. The plane is loaded with sensors that give the pilot real-time information. A high-speed data link allows the plane to communicate with other planes and with contacts on the ground.

Drone aircraft will change the way the military carries out missions. Drones of the future will be smaller, faster, and smarter than ever. Swarms of small drones controlled by artificial intelligence (AI) could communicate like a swarm of insects. Together, the drones could make and carry out plans and then adjust to changing conditions, all without the help of people.

▲

AI WILL DETERMINE
HOW DRONES WORK TOGETHER
BASED ON BATTLE CONDITIONS.

Military Tech in Action

Imagine that a group of US troops is trapped and needs help. They're too far away for a helicopter to reach in time, and there's no place nearby for a jet to land.

Situations like this one inspired the US military's V-22 Osprey. This aircraft flies like an airplane. But it can take off and land like a helicopter. An Osprey pilot can tilt the plane's rotors so the plane can touch down on rough terrain.

This Osprey is tilting its rotors into flight position.

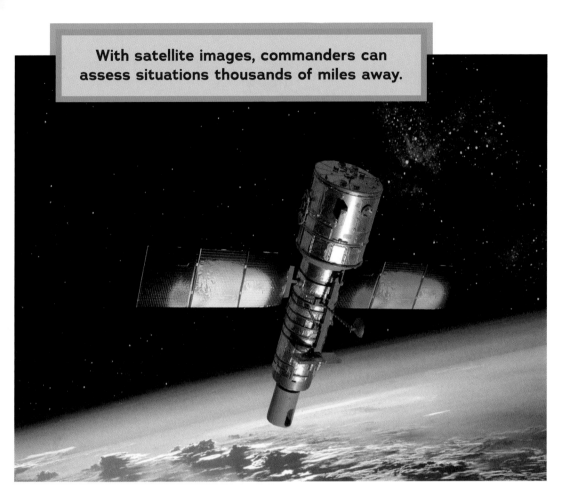

With satellite images, commanders can assess situations thousands of miles away.

Space Race

Some experts believe future military actions will take place in space. For some countries, the race to create a military presence in space has begun. Already, military satellites orbit Earth. These satellites can photograph almost any part of the world. They provide the military with the detailed, real-time information commanders need to make important decisions.

A nuclear attack is one of the biggest threats a nation could face. But space-based missile defense systems might be able to stop an attack before it happens. The US military hopes to develop lasers that can shoot down missiles. The lasers could attach to satellites orbiting Earth. They could also attach to drones that stay 60,000 feet (18,288 m) above the ground, close to the edge of space.

The US military tests missiles at sea, far from land and people.

THE FIRST SPACE SHUTTLE WAS 184 FEET (56 M) LONG. THE X-37B IS ONLY 29 FEET (8.8 M).

The US military is also exploring space planes. The US Air Force already has a plane in space, the X-37B mini shuttle. What the air force does with the X-37B is top secret. People can only guess what its mission is. But we do know that this unpiloted shuttle can stay in space for a year or more. Then it can return to Earth safely, landing like a regular plane.

Coding Spotlight

AI allows drone vehicles to perform tasks, react, and respond to their environment. Coding AI software is a big task. Four different layers of AI must work together.

First, the AI must be able to sense its environment. Second, it needs to use the data from its sensors to create a picture of its surroundings. Third, it needs machine learning, or the ability to solve problems. Finally, deep learning allows the AI to solve problems more effectively in the future.

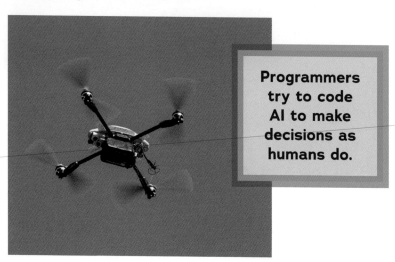

Programmers try to code AI to make decisions as humans do.

Chapter 4

THE FUTURE OF WARFARE

What will warfare look like in twenty, fifty, or even one hundred years? No one knows. But based on the latest technology, we can guess.

What if commanders could know just how tired or stressed their soldiers are? That's one reason for biosensors. Future soldiers might wear sensors that monitor their health and emotions. These sensors could warn commanders when their troops are at risk of making mistakes.

Outside the military, many people wear sensors to monitor things such as heart rate or the number of steps they take.

Using virtual reality, soldiers can train for a wide variety of situations.

Military tech is already linking humans and technology. In the future, soldiers may have computers wired directly into their minds and bodies. The science behind these connections is called cybernetics. With computers connected to their brains, soldiers could access unlimited information. Mechanical limbs, high-tech exoskeletons, and other artificial body parts could make soldiers almost invulnerable.

New implants could boost soldiers' abilities. The US military is exploring brain implants that improve soldiers' memories. Other implanted devices could sharpen soldiers' eyesight, hearing, or reflexes.

Possibly, future warfare won't include people at all. Militaries around the world are building up their drone and AI forces. Advances in technology could mean that robot soldiers go into battle instead of humans. A super-intelligent AI commander could give them their orders.

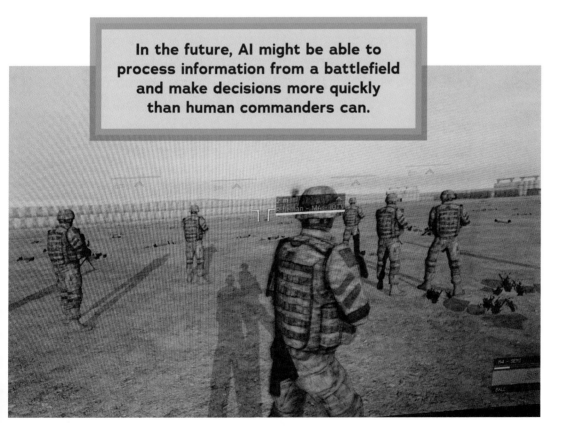

In the future, AI might be able to process information from a battlefield and make decisions more quickly than human commanders can.

Science Fact or Science Fiction?

Robots make better soldiers than human beings do.

It's fiction!

Robots have many advantages over human beings. They're stronger, don't get tired, and never feel afraid. But they're no substitute for people. Though programmers are constantly improving AI, it currently lacks the problem-solving abilities humans have. AI cannot adapt as easily to new situations. Humans are much better at decision-making, an important skill to have in battle.

Maybe one day the idea of war will be something from the past. People might learn to solve their differences peacefully. But until that day arrives, militaries around the globe will continue to develop the latest, greatest technology to give them the edge in battle.

The future of military technology could be something no one has imagined yet.

Glossary

augmented reality: computer-made images and data that are projected over a user's view of the real world

camouflage: to hide from view by blending into the surroundings

cybernetics: the science of combining technology with living things

drone: a vehicle that has no driver or pilot

exoskeleton: a hard structure on the outside of the body

infrared: a type of invisible light experienced by humans as heat

precision: how accurate something is

real-time: the actual time something is happening

rotor: spinning blades that lift and move an aircraft such as a helicopter

sensor: a small computer device that detects or measures something

stealth: the ability to hide from view

Learn More about Military Technology

Books

Hagler, Gina. *The Evolution of Military Technology.* New York: Britannica/
Rosen, 2019. Follow the evolution of military technology from ancient
to modern times.

Leigh, Anna. *How Drones Work.* Minneapolis: Lerner Publications, 2020.
Learn more about the history of drones, how they're built, and the
technology behind them.

Ulh, Xina M. *Using Computer Science in Military Service.* New York: Rosen
YA, 2019. From robots to drones, learn how computer science helps
create the latest military technology.

Websites

Ducksters: US Armed Forces
https://www.ducksters.com/history/us_government/united_states
_armed_forces.php
Get an overview of each branch of the US military.

Facts about Drones
https://mocomi.com/drones/
Curious about drones? Watch this video to learn more.

Military Aircraft for Kids
http://bambo-jambo.com/military-equipment/military-aircraft-for-kids/
Discover different types of military aircraft in this video.

Index

Photo Acknowledgments

Image credits: Chesky_W/Getty Images, p. 4; U.S. Navy/Lt. Cmdr. Michael Smith/, p. 5; U.S. Marine Corps/Cpl. Ariana Acosta, p. 6; U.S. Navy/Mass Communication Specialist 2nd Class Daniel Rolston, p. 7; BAE Systems, p. 8; U.S. Navy/John F. Williams, p. 9; U.S. Navy/Rebecca Eckhoff, p. 10; U.S. Air National Guard/Tech. Sgt. Ryan Campbell, p. 11; Lockheed Martin Corporation, p. 12; U.S. Army/Sgt. William Battle, p. 13; Fadel Senna/AFP/Getty Images, p. 14; U.S. Air Force/Tech. Sgt. Gregory Brook, p. 15; Sandia National Laboratories/Randy Montoya, p. 16; U.S. Marine Corps/Sgt. Alex Kouns, p. 17; U.S. Air Force/Navy Chief Petty Officer Shannon E. Renfroe, p. 18; DARPA, p. 19; U.S. Marine Corps/Cpl. A. J. Van Fredenberg, p. 20; Erik Simonsen/Getty Images, p. 21; U.S. Navy/Mass Communication Specialist 1st Class Ronald Gutridge, p. 22; Jason Connolly/AFP/Getty Images, p. 23; U.S. Marine Corps/Cpl. Melanye Martinez, p. 24; Pavel Korotkov/Shutterstock.com, p. 25; U.S. Army/Pfc. Samantha J. Whitehead, p. 26; U.S. Army National Guard/Master Sgt. Paul Wade, p. 27; onurdongel/Getty Images, p. 28; Colin Anderson Productions pty ltd/Getty Images, p. 29.

Cover: U.S. Marines/Lance Cpl. Dalton S. Swanbeck.